I0481958

# WASHINGTON RULES OF EVIDENCE 2018

This edition of the Washington Rules of Evidence 2018 contains the complete rules as revised through January 1, 2018.

ISBN-13: 978-1721991389

ISBN-10: 1721991387

Washington Legal Publishing, LLC

# Table of Contents

## Title 1 General Provisions
### RULE ER 101. SCOPE

These rules govern proceedings in the courts of the state of Washington to the extent and with the exceptions stated in rule 1101.

[Adopted effective April 2, 1979]

Comment 101

[Deleted effective September 1, 2006.]

### RULE ER 102. PURPOSE AND CONSTRUCTION

These rules shall be construed to secure fairness in administration, elimination of unjustifiable expense and delay, and promotion of growth and development of the law of evidence to the end that the truth may be ascertained and proceedings justly determined.

[Adopted effective April 2, 1979]

Comment 102

[Deleted effective September 1, 2006.]

(a)  Effect of Erroneous Ruling.  Error may not be predicated upon a ruling which admits or excludes evidence unless a substantial right of the party is affected, and

(1)  Objection.  In case the ruling is one admitting evidence, a timely objection or motion to strike is made, stating the specific ground of objection, if the specific ground was not apparent from the context; or

(2)  Offer of Proof.  In case the ruling is one excluding evidence, the substance of the evidence was made  known to the court by offer or was apparent from the context within which questions were asked.

(b)  Record of Offer and Ruling.  The court may add any other or further statement which shows the character of the evidence, the form in which it was offered, the objection made, and the ruling thereon. The court may direct the making of an offer in question and answer form.

(c)  Hearing of Jury.  In jury cases, proceedings shall be conducted, to the extent practicable, so as to prevent inadmissible evidence from being suggested to the jury by any means, such as making statements or offers of proof or asking questions in the hearing of the jury.

(d)  Errors Raised for the First Time on Review. [Reserved - See RAP 2.5(a).]

[Adopted effective April 2, 1979]

Comment 103

[Deleted effective September 1, 2006.]

## RULE ER 104. PRELIMINARY QUESTIONS

(a)   Questions   of   Admissibility   Generally. Preliminary questions concerning the qualification of a person to be a witness, the existence of a privilege, or the admissibility of evidence shall be determined by the court, subject to the provisions of section (b). In making its determination it is not bound by the Rules of Evidence except those with respect to privileges.

(b)  Relevancy  Conditioned  on  Fact.  When  the relevancy of evidence depends upon the fulfillment of a condition of fact, the court shall admit it upon, or subject to, the introduction of evidence sufficient to support a finding of the fulfillment of the condition.

(c) Hearing of Jury. Hearings on the admissibility of confessions shall in all cases be conducted out of the hearing of the jury. Hearings on other preliminary matters shall be so conducted when the interests of justice require or, when an accused is a witness and so requests.

(d) Testimony by Accused. The accused does not, by testifying upon a preliminary matter, become subject to cross examination as to other issues in the case.

(e)  Weight  and  Credibility.  This  rule  does  not limit the right of a party to introduce before the jury evidence relevant to weight or credibility.

[Amended effective September 1, 1992.]

Comment 104

[Deleted effective September 1, 2006.]

## RULE ER 105. LIMITED ADMISSIBILITY

When evidence which is admissible as to one party or for one purpose but not admissible as to another party or for another purpose is admitted, the court, upon request, shall restrict the evidence to its proper scope and instruct the jury accordingly.

[[Adopted effective April 2, 1979.]

Comment 105

[Deleted effective September 1, 2006.]

## RULE ER 106. REMAINDER OF OR RELATED WRITINGS OR RECORDED STATEMENTS

When a writing or recorded statement or part thereof is introduced by a party, an adverse party may require the party at that time to introduce any other part, or any other writing or recorded statement, which ought in fairness to be considered contemporaneously with it.

[Adopted effective April 2, 1979.]

Comment 106

[Deleted effective September 1, 2006.]

(a) Scope of Rule. This rule governs only judicial notice of adjudicative facts.

(b) Kinds of Facts. A judicially noticed fact must be one not subject to reasonable dispute in that it is either (1) generally known within the territorial jurisdiction of the trial court or (2) capable of accurate and ready determination by resort to sources whose accuracy cannot reasonably be questioned.

(c) When Discretionary. A court may take judicial notice, whether requested or not.

(d) When Mandatory. A court shall take judicial notice if requested by a party and supplied with the necessary information.

(e) Opportunity To Be Heard. A party is entitled upon timely request to an opportunity to be heard as to the propriety of taking judicial notice and the tenor of the matter noticed. In the absence of prior notification, the request may be made after judicial notice has been taken.

(f) Time of Taking Notice. Judicial notice may be taken at any stage of the proceeding.

[Adopted effective April 2, 1979.]

Comment 201

[Deleted effective September 1, 2006.]

# Title 3 Presumptions in Civil Actions and Proceedings

(RESERVED)

[Adopted effective April 2, 1979.]

Comment 301

[Deleted effective September 1, 2006.]

## RULE ER 302. APPLICABILITY OF STATE LAW IN CIVIL ACTIONS AND PROCEEDINGS

[RESERVED]

[Adopted effective April 2, 1979.]

Comment 302

[Deleted effective September 1, 2006.]

"Relevant evidence" means evidence having any tendency to make the existence of any fact that is of consequence to the determination of the action more probable or less probable than it would be without the evidence.

[Adopted effective April 2, 1979.]

Comment 401

[Deleted effective September 1, 2006.]

### RULE ER 402. RELEVANT EVIDENCE GENERALLY ADMISSIBLE; IRRELEVANT EVIDENCE INADMISSIBLE

All relevant evidence is admissible, except as limited by constitutional requirements or as otherwise provided by statute, by these rules, or by other rules or regulations applicable in the courts of this state. Evidence which is not relevant is not admissible.

[Adopted effective April 2, 1979.]

Comment 402

[Deleted effective September 1, 2006.]

### RULE ER 403. EXCLUSION OF RELEVANT EVIDENCE ON GROUNDS OF PREJUDICE, CONFUSION, OR WASTE OF TIME

Although relevant, evidence may be excluded if its probative value is substantially outweighed by the danger of unfair prejudice, confusion of the issues, or misleading the jury, or by considerations of undue delay, waste of time, or needless presentation of cumulative evidence.

[Adopted effective April 2, 1979.]

Comment 403

[Deleted effective September 1, 2006.]

## RULE ER 404. CHARACTER EVIDENCE NOT ADMISSIBLE TO PROVE CONDUCT; EXCEPTIONS; OTHER CRIMES

(a) Character Evidence Generally. Evidence of a person's character or a trait of character is not admissible for the purpose of proving action in conformity therewith on a particular occasion, except:

(1) Character of Accused. Evidence of a pertinent trait of character offered by an accused, or by the prosecution to rebut the same;

(2) Character of Victim. Evidence of a pertinent trait of character of the victim of the crime offered by an accused, or by the prosecution to rebut the same, or evidence of a character trait of peacefulness of the victim offered by the prosecution in a homicide case to rebut evidence that the victim was the first aggressor;

(3) Character of Witness. Evidence of the character of a witness, as provided in rules 607, 608, and 609.

(b) Other Crimes, Wrongs, or Acts. Evidence of other crimes, wrongs, or acts is not admissible to prove the character of a person in order to show action in conformity therewith. It may, however, be admissible for other purposes, such as proof of motive, opportunity, intent, preparation, plan, knowledge, identity, or absence of mistake or accident.

[Amended effective September 1, 1992.]

Comment 404

[Deleted effective September 1, 2006.]

## RULE ER 405. METHODS OF PROVING CHARACTER

(a) Reputation. In all cases in which evidence of character or a trait of character of a person is admissible, proof may be made by testimony as to reputation. On cross examination, inquiry is allowable into relevant specific instances of conduct.

(b) Specific Instances of Conduct. In cases in which character or a trait of character of a person is an essential element of a charge, claim, or defense, proof may also be made of specific instances of that person's conduct.

[Amended effective September 1, 1992.]

Comment 405

[Deleted effective September 1, 2006.]

## RULE ER 406. HABIT; ROUTINE PRACTICE

Evidence of the habit of a person or of the routine practice of an organization, whether corroborated or not and regardless of the presence of eyewitnesses, is relevant to prove that the conduct of the person or organization on a particular occasion was in conformity with the habit or routine practice.

[Adopted effective April 2, 1979.]

Comment 406

[Deleted effective September 1, 2006.]

## RULE ER 407. SUBSEQUENT REMEDIAL MEASURES

When, after an event, measures are taken which, if taken previously, would have made the event less likely to occur, evidence of the subsequent measures is not admissible to prove negligence or culpable conduct in connection with the event. This rule does not require the exclusion of evidence of subsequent measures when offered for another purpose, such as proving ownership, control, or feasibility of precautionary measures, if controverted, or impeachment.

[Adopted effective April 2, 1979.]

Comment 407

[Deleted effective September 1, 2006.]

## RULE ER 408. COMPROMISE AND OFFERS TO COMPROMISE

In a civil case, evidence of (1) furnishing or offering or promising to furnish, or (2) accepting or offering or promising to accept a valuable consideration in compromising or attempting to compromise a claim which was disputed as to either validity or amount, is not admissible to prove liability for or invalidity of the claim or its amount. Evidence of conduct or statements made in compromise negotiations is likewise not admissible. This rule does not require exclusion of any evidence otherwise discoverable merely because it is presented in the course of compromise negotiations. This rule also does not require exclusion when the evidence is offered for another purpose, such as proving bias or prejudice of a witness, negating a contention of undue delay, or proving an effort to obstruct a criminal investigation or prosecution.

[Adopted effective April 2, 1979; amended effective September 1, 2008]

### Comment 408

[Deleted effective September 1, 2006.]

## RULE ER 409. PAYMENT OF MEDICAL AND SIMILAR EXPENSES

Evidence of furnishing or offering or promising to pay medical, hospital, or similar expenses occasioned by an injury is not admissible to prove liability for the injury.

[Adopted effective April 2, 1979.]

Comment 409

[Deleted effective September 1, 2006.]

## RULE ER 410. INADMISSIBILITY OF PLEAS, OFFERS OF PLEAS, AND RELATED STATEMENTS

(a) General. Except as otherwise provided in this rule, evidence of a plea of guilty, later withdrawn, or a plea of nolo contendere, or of an offer to plead guilty or nolo contendere to the crime charged or any other crime, or of statements made in connection with, and relevant to, any of the foregoing pleas or offers, is not admissible in any civil or criminal proceeding against the person who made the plea or offer. However, evidence of a statement made in connection with, and relevant to, a plea of guilty, later withdrawn, a plea of nolo contendere, or an offer to plead guilty or nolo contendere to the crime charged or any other crime, is admissible in a criminal proceeding for perjury or false statement if the statement was made by the defendant under oath and in the presence of counsel. This rule does not govern the admissibility of evidence of a deferred sentence imposed under RCW 3.66.067 or RCW 9.95.200-.240.

(b) Statutory Offers of Compromise. Evidence of payment or an offer or agreement to pay (i) to compromise a misdemeanor pursuant to RCW Chapter 10.22, or (ii) for a liability described in RCW 4.24.230, shall not be admissible in any civil or criminal proceeding.

[Adopted effective April 2, 1979. Amended effective September 1, 2008]

Comment 410

[Deleted effective September 1, 2006.]

## RULE ER 411. LIABILITY INSURANCE

Evidence that a person was or was not insured against liability is not admissible upon the issue whether the person acted negligently or otherwise wrongfully. This rule does not require the exclusion of evidence of insurance against liability when offered for another purpose, such as proof of agency, ownership, or control, or bias or prejudice of a witness.

[Amended effective September 1, 1992.]

Comment 411

[Deleted effective September 1, 2006.]

## RULE ER 412. SEXUAL OFFENSES - VICTIM'S PAST BEHAVIOR

(a)       Criminal Cases.   [Reserved.    See RCW 9A.44.020.]

(b)  Civil Cases; Evidence Generally Inadmissible. The following evidence is not admissible in any civil proceeding involving alleged sexual misconduct except as provided in sections (c) and (d):

(1)  Evidence offered to prove that any alleged victim engaged in other sexual behavior.

(2)  Evidence offered to prove any alleged victim's sexual predisposition.

(c) Exceptions. In a civil case, evidence offered to prove the sexual behavior or sexual predisposition of any alleged victim is admissible if it is otherwise admissible under these rules and its probative value substantially outweighs the danger of harm to any victim and of unfair prejudice to any party. Evidence of an alleged victim's reputation is admissible only if it has been placed in controversy by the alleged victim.

(d) Procedure to determine admissibility.

(1) A party intending to offer evidence under section (c) must:

(A) file a written motion at least 14 days before trial specifically describing the evidence and stating the purpose for which it is offered unless the court, for good cause, requires a different time for filing or permits filing during trial; and

(B) serve the motion on all parties and notify the alleged victim or, when appropriate, the alleged victim's guardian or representative.

(2) Before admitting evidence under this rule the court must conduct a hearing in camera and afford the victim and parties a right to attend and be heard. The motion, related papers, and the record of the hearing must be sealed and remain under seal unless the court orders otherwise.

[Adopted effective September 1, 1988.]


Comment 412

[Deleted effective September 1, 2003.]

The following citations are to certain statutes that make reference to privileges or privileged communications. This list is not intended to create any privilege, nor to abrogate any privilege by implication or omission.

(a)     Attorney-Client.     (Reserved.     See     RCW 5.60.060(2).)

(b)     Clergyman    or    Priest.    (Reserved.    See    RCW 5.60.060(3), 26.44.060, 70.124.060.)

(c)     Dispute    Resolution    Center.    (Reserved.  See  RCW 7.75.050.)

(d)     Counselor. (Reserved. See RCW 18.19.180.)

(e)     Higher Education Procedures. (Reserved. See RCW 28B.19.120(4).)

(f)     Spouse or Domestic Partner.    (Reserved. See RCW 5.60.060(1), 26.20.071, 26.21A275(8).)

(g)     Interpreter in Legal Proceeding. (Reserved. See RCW 2.42.160; GR 11.1(e).)

(h)     Journalist. (Reserved.  See RCW 5.68.010.)

(i)     Optometrist-Patient.     (Reserved.     See     RCW 18.53.200, 26.44.060.)

(j)     Physician-Patient.     (Reserved.     See     RCW 5.60.060(4), 26.26.120, 26.44.060, 51.04.050,
        69.41.020, 69.50.403, 70.124.060, 71.05.250.)

(k)   Psychologist-Client.   (Reserved.   See   RCW 18.83.110, 26.44.060, 70.124.060.)

(l) Public Assistance Recipient. (Reserved. See RCW 74.04.060.)

(m)   Public   Officer.   (Reserved.   See   RCW 5.60.060(5).)

(n) Registered Nurse. (Reserved. See RCW 5.62.010, 5.62.020, 5.62.030.)


[Adopted effective September 1, 1988; amended effective September 1, 1992; January 4, 2005; September 1, 2012.]


Comment 501

[Deleted effective September 1, 2006.]

## RULE ER 502. ATTORNEY-CLIENT PRIVILEGE AND WORK PRODUCT; LIMITATIONS ON WAIVER


The   following   provisions   apply,   in   the circumstances set out, to disclosure of a communication or information covered by the attorney-client privilege or work-product protection.

(a) Disclosure Made in a Washington Proceeding or to a Washington Office or Agency; Scope of a Waiver. When the disclosure is made in a Washington proceeding or to a Washington office or agency and waives the attorney-client privilege or work-product protection, the waiver extends to an undisclosed communication or information in any proceeding only if:

(1)  the waiver is intentional;

(2) the disclosed and undisclosed communications or information concern
the same subject matter; and

(3) they should, in fairness, be considered together.

(b) Inadvertent Disclosure. When made in a Washington proceeding or to a Washington office or agency, the disclosure does not operate as a waiver in any proceeding if:

(1) the disclosure is inadvertent;

(2) the holder of the privilege or protection took reasonable steps to prevent disclosure; and

(3) the holder promptly took reasonable steps to rectify the error, including (if applicable) following CR 26(b)(6).

(c) Disclosure Made in a Non-Washington Proceeding. When the disclosure is made in a non-Washington proceeding and is not the subject of a court order concerning waiver, the disclosure does not operate as a waiver in a Washington proceeding if the disclosure:

(1) would not be a waiver under this rule if it had been made in Washington proceeding; or

(2) is not a waiver under the law of the jurisdiction where the disclosure occurred.

(d) Controlling Effect of a Court Order. A Washington court may order that the privilege or protection is not waived by disclosure connected with the litigation pending before the court-in which event the disclosure is also not a waiver in any other proceeding.

(e) Controlling Effect of a Party Agreement. An agreement on the effect of disclosure in a Washington proceeding is binding only on the parties to the agreement, unless it is incorporated into a court order.

(f) Definitions. In this rule:

(1) "attorney-client privilege" means the protection that applicable law provides for confidential attorney-client communications; and

(2) "work-product protection" means the protection that applicable law provides for tangible material (or its intangible equivalent) prepared in anticipation of litigation or for trial.

[Adopted effective September 1, 2010]

## RULE ER 601. GENERAL RULE OF COMPETENCY

Every person is competent to be a witness except as otherwise provided by statute or by court rule.

[Adopted effective April 2, 1979.]

Comment 601

[Deleted effective September 1, 2006.]

## RULE ER 602. LACK OF PERSONAL KNOWLEDGE

A witness may not testify to a matter unless evidence is introduced sufficient to support a finding that the witness has personal knowledge of the matter. Evidence to prove personal knowledge may, but need not, consist of the witness' own testimony. This rule is subject to the provisions of rule 703, relating to opinion testimony by expert witnesses.

[Amended effective September 1, 1992.]

Comment 602

[Deleted effective September 1, 2006.]

## RULE ER 603. OATH OR AFFIRMATION

Before testifying, every witness shall be required to declare that the witness will testify truthfully, by

oath or affirmation administered in a form calculated
to awaken the witness' conscience and impress the
witness' mind with the duty to do so.


[Amended effective September 1, 1992.]


Comment 603

[Deleted effective September 1, 2006.]

## RULE ER 604. INTERPRETERS


An interpreter is subject to the provisions of
these rules relating to qualification as an expert and
the administration of an oath or affirmation to make a
true translation.


[Amended effective September 1, 1992.]


Comment 604

[Deleted effective September 1, 2006.]

## RULE ER 605. COMPETENCY OF JUDGE AS WITNESS


The judge presiding at the trial may not testify in
that trial as a witness. No objection need be made in
order to preserve the point.


[Adopted effective April 2, 1979.]


Comment 605

[Deleted effective September 1, 2006.]

## RULE ER 606. COMPETENCY OF JUROR AS WITNESS

A member of the jury may not testify as a witness before that jury in the trial of the case in which the juror is sitting. If the juror is called so to testify, the opposing party shall be afforded an opportunity to object out of the presence of the jury.

[Amended effective September 1, 1992.]

Comment 606

[Deleted effective September 1, 2006.]

## RULE ER 607. WHO MAY IMPEACH

The credibility of a witness may be attacked by any party, including the party calling the witness.

[Amended effective September 1, 1992.]

Comment 607

[Deleted effective September 1, 2006.]

## RULE ER 608. EVIDENCE OF CHARACTER AND CONDUCT OF WITNESS

(a) Reputation Evidence of Character. The credibility of a witness may be attacked or supported by evidence in the form of reputation, but subject to the limitations: (1) the evidence may refer only to character for truthfulness or untruthfulness, and (2) evidence of truthful character is admissible only after the character of the witness for truthfulness has been attacked by reputation evidence or otherwise.

(b) Specific Instances of Conduct. Specific instances of the conduct of a witness, for the purpose of attacking or supporting the witness' credibility, other than conviction of crime as provided in rule 609, may not be proved by extrinsic evidence. They may, however, in the discretion of the court, if probative of truthfulness or untruthfulness, be inquired into on cross examination of the witness (1) concerning the witness' character for truthfulness or untruthfulness, or (2) concerning the character for truthfulness or untruthfulness of another witness as to which character the witness being cross-examined has testified.

[Amended effective September 1, 1992.]

Comment 608

[Deleted effective September 1, 2006.]

## RULE ER 609. IMPEACHMENT BY EVIDENCE OF CONVICTION OF CRIME

(a) General Rule. For the purpose of attacking the credibility of a witness in a criminal or civil case, evidence that the witness has been convicted of a crime shall be admitted if elicited from the witness or established by public record during examination of the witness but only if the crime (1) was punishable by death or imprisonment in excess of 1 year under the law under which the witness was convicted, and the court determines that the probative value of admitting

26

this evidence outweighs the prejudice to the party against whom the evidence is offered, or (2) involved dishonesty or false statement, regardless of the punishment.

(b) Time Limit. Evidence of a conviction under this rule is not admissible if a period of more than 10 years has elapsed since the date of the conviction or of the release of the witness from the confinement imposed for that conviction, whichever is the later date, unless the court determines, in the interests of justice, that the probative value of the conviction supported by specific facts and circumstances substantially outweighs its prejudicial effect. However, evidence of a conviction more than 10 years old as calculated herein, is not admissible unless the proponent gives to the adverse party sufficient advance written notice of intent to use such evidence to provide the adverse party with a fair opportunity to contest the use of such evidence.

(c) Effect of Pardon, Annulment, or Certificate of Rehabilitation. Evidence of a conviction is not admissible under this rule if (1) the conviction has been the subject of a pardon, annulment, certificate of rehabilitation, or other equivalent procedure based on a finding of the rehabilitation of the person convicted, and that person has not been convicted of a subsequent crime which was punishable by death or imprisonment in excess of 1 year, or (2) the conviction has been the subject of a pardon, annulment, or other equivalent procedure based on a finding of innocence.

(d) Juvenile Adjudications. Evidence of juvenile adjudications is generally not admissible under this rule. The court may, however, in a criminal case allow evidence of a finding of guilt in a juvenile offense proceeding of a witness other than the accused if conviction of the offense would be admissible to attack the credibility of an adult and the court is satisfied that admission in evidence is necessary for a fair determination of the issue of guilt or innocence.

(e) Pendency of Appeal. The pendency of an appeal therefrom does not render evidence of a conviction inadmissible. Evidence of the pendency of an appeal is admissible.

[Amended effective September 1, 1988

Comment 609

[Deleted effective September 1, 2006.]

## RULE ER 610. RELIGIOUS BELIEFS OR OPINIONS

Evidence of the beliefs or opinions of a witness on matters of religion is not admissible for the purpose of showing that by reason of their nature the witness' credibility is impaired or enhanced.

[Amended effective September 1, 1992.]

Comment 610

[Deleted effective September 1, 2006.]

## RULE ER 611. MODE AND ORDER OF INTERROGATION AND PRESENTATION

(a) Control by Court. The court shall exercise reasonable control over the mode and order of interrogating witnesses and presenting evidence so as to (1) make the interrogation and presentation effective for the ascertainment of the truth, (2) avoid needless consumption of time, and (3) protect witnesses from harassment or undue embarrassment.

(b) Scope of Cross Examination. Cross examination should be limited to the subject matter of the direct examination and matters affecting the credibility of the witness. The court may, in the exercise of discretion, permit inquiry into additional matters as if on direct examination.

(c) Leading Questions. Leading questions should not be used on the direct examination of a witness except as may be necessary to develop the witness' testimony. Ordinarily leading questions should be permitted on cross examination. When a party calls a hostile witness, an adverse party, or a witness identified with an adverse party, interrogation may be by leading questions.

[Amended effective September 1, 1992.]

Comment 611

[Deleted effective September 1, 2006.]

## RULE ER 612. WRITING USED TO REFRESH MEMORY

If a witness uses a writing to refresh memory for the purpose of testifying, either: while testifying, or before testifying, if the court in its discretion determines it is necessary in the interests of justice, an adverse party is entitled to have the writing produced at the hearing, to inspect it, to cross-examine the witness thereon, and to introduce in evidence those portions which relate to the testimony of the witness. If it is claimed that the writing contains matters not related to the subject matter of the testimony, the court shall examine the writing in camera, excise any portions not so related, and order delivery of the remainder to the party entitled thereto. Any portion withheld over objections shall be preserved and made available to the appellate court in the event of an appeal. If a writing is not produced or delivered pursuant to order under this rule, the court shall make any order justice requires.

[Amended effective September 1, 1992.]

Comment 612

[Deleted effective September 1, 2006.]

## RULE ER 613. PRIOR STATEMENTS OF WITNESSES

(a) Examining Witness Concerning Prior Statement. In the examination of a witness concerning a prior statement made by the witness, whether written or not, the court may require that the statement be shown or its contents disclosed to the witness at that time, and on request the same shall be shown or disclosed to opposing counsel.

(b) Extrinsic Evidence of Prior Inconsistent Statement of Witness. Extrinsic evidence of a prior inconsistent statement by a witness is not admissible unless the witness is afforded an opportunity to explain or deny the same and the opposite party is afforded an opportunity to interrogate the witness thereon, or the interests of justice otherwise require. This provision does not apply to admissions of a party-opponent as defined in rule 801(d)(2).

[Amended effective September 1, 1992.]


Comment 613

[Deleted effective September 1, 2006.]

## RULE ER 614. CALLING AND INTERROGATION OF WITNESSES BY COURT


(a) Calling by Court. The court may, on its own motion where necessary in the interests of justice or on motion of a party, call witnesses, and all parties are entitled to cross-examine witnesses thus called.

(b) Interrogation by Court. The court may interrogate witnesses, whether called by itself or by a party; provided, however, that in trials before a jury, the court's questioning must be cautiously guarded so as not to constitute a comment on the evidence.

(c) Objections. Objections to the calling of witnesses by the court or to interrogation by it may be made at the time or at the next available opportunity when the jury is not present.


[Adopted effective April 2, 1979.]


Comment 614

[Deleted effective September 1, 2006.]

## RULE ER 615. EXCLUSION OF WITNESSES


At the request of a party the court may order witnesses excluded so that they cannot hear the testimony of other witnesses, and it may make the order of its own motion. This rule does not authorize exclusion of (1) a party who is a natural person, or (2) an officer or employee of a party which is not a natural person designated as its representative by its attorney, or (3) a person whose presence is shown by a party to be reasonably necessary to the presentation of the party's cause.


[Amended effective September 1, 1992.]


Comment 615

[Deleted effective September 1, 2006.]

If the witness is not testifying as an expert, the witness' testimony in the form of opinions or inferences is limited to those opinions or inferences which are (a) rationally based on the perception of the witness, (b) helpful to a clear understanding of the witness' testimony or the determination of a fact in issue, and (c) not based on scientific, technical, or other specialized knowledge within the scope of rule 702.

[Amended effective September 1, 1992; September 1, 2004.]

Comment 701

[Deleted effective September 1, 2006.]

### RULE ER 702. TESTIMONY BY EXPERTS

If scientific, technical, or other specialized knowledge will assist the trier of fact to understand the evidence or to determine a fact in issue, a witness qualified as an expert by knowledge, skill, experience, training, or education, may testify thereto in the form of an opinion or otherwise.

[Adopted effective April 2, 1979.]

Comment 702

[Deleted effective September 1, 2006.]

## RULE ER 703. BASES OF OPINION TESTIMONY BY EXPERTS

The facts or data in the particular case upon which an expert bases an opinion or inference may be those perceived by or made known to the expert at or before the hearing. If of a type reasonably relied upon by experts in the particular field in forming opinions or inferences upon the subject, the facts or data need not be admissible in evidence.

[Amended effective September 1, 1992.]

Comment 703

[Deleted effective September 1, 2006.]

## RULE ER 704. OPINION ON ULTIMATE ISSUE

Testimony in the form of an opinion or inferences otherwise admissible is not objectionable because it embraces an ultimate issue to be decided by the trier of fact.

[Adopted effective April 2, 1979.]

Comment 704

[Deleted effective September 1, 2006.]

The expert may testify in terms of opinion or inference and give reasons therefor without prior disclosure of the underlying facts or data, unless the judge requires otherwise. The expert may in any event be required to disclose the underlying facts or data on cross examination.

[Amended effective September 1, 1992.]

Comment 705

[Deleted effective September 1, 2006.]

(a) Appointment. The court may on its own motion or on the motion of any party enter an order to show cause why expert witnesses should not be appointed, and may request the parties to submit nominations. The court may appoint any expert witnesses agreed upon by the parties, and may appoint witnesses of its own selection. An expert witness shall not be appointed by the court unless the witness consents to act. A witness so appointed shall be informed of the witness' duties by the court in writing, a copy of which shall be filed with the clerk, or at a conference in which the parties shall have opportunity to participate. A witness so appointed shall advise the parties of the witness' findings, if any; the witness' deposition may be taken by any party; and the witness may be called to testify by the court or any party. The witness shall be subject to cross examination by each party, including a party calling the witness.

(b) Compensation. Expert witnesses so appointed are entitled to reasonable compensation in whatever sum the court may allow. Except as otherwise provided by law, the compensation shall be paid by the parties in such proportion and at such time as the court directs, and thereafter charged in like manner as other costs.

(c) Disclosure of Appointment. In the exercise of its discretion, the court may authorize disclosure to the jury of the fact that the court appointed the expert witness.

(d) Parties' Experts of Own Selection. Nothing in this rule limits the parties in calling expert witnesses of their own selection.

[Amended effective September 1, 1992.]

Comment 706

[Deleted effective September 1, 2006.]

The following definitions apply under this article:

(a) Statement. A "statement" is (1) an oral or written assertion or (2) nonverbal conduct of a person, if it is intended by the person as an assertion.

(b) Declarant. A "declarant" is a person who makes a statement.

(c) Hearsay. "Hearsay" is a statement, other than one made by the declarant while testifying at the trial or hearing, offered in evidence to prove the truth of the matter asserted.

(d) Statements Which Are Not Hearsay. A statement is not hearsay if--

(1) Prior Statement by Witness. The declarant testifies at the trial or hearing and is subject to cross examination concerning the statement, and the statement is (i) inconsistent with the declarant's testimony, and was given under oath subject to the penalty of perjury at a trial, hearing, or other proceeding, or in a deposition, or (ii) consistent with the declarant's testimony and is offered to rebut an express or implied charge against the declarant of recent fabrication or improper influence or motive, or (iii) one of identification of a person made after perceiving the person; or

(2) Admission by Party-Opponent. The statement is offered against a party and is (i) the party's own statement, in either an individual or a representative capacity or (ii) a statement of which the party has manifested an adoption or belief in its truth, or (iii) a statement by a person authorized by the party to make a statement concerning the subject, or (iv) a statement

by the party's agent or servant acting within the scope of the authority to make the statement for the party, or (v) a statement by a coconspirator of a party during the course and in furtherance of the conspiracy.

[Amended effective September 1, 1992.]

## Comment 801

[Deleted effective September 1, 2006.]

## RULE ER 802. HEARSAY RULE

Hearsay is not admissible except as provided by these rules, by other court rules, or by statute.

[Adopted effective April 2, 1979.]

## Comment 802

[Deleted effective September 1, 2006.]

## RULE ER 803. HEARSAY EXCEPTIONS; AVAILABILITY OF DECLARANT IMMATERIAL

(a) Specific Exceptions. The following are not excluded by the hearsay rule, even though the declarant is available as a witness:

(1) Present Sense Impression. A statement describing or explaining an event or condition made while the declarant was perceiving the event or condition, or immediately thereafter.

(2) Excited Utterance. A statement relating to a startling event or condition made while the declarant was under the stress of excitement caused by the event or condition.

(3) Then Existing Mental, Emotional, or Physical Condition. A statement of the declarant's then existing state of mind, emotion, sensation, or physical condition (such as intent, plan, motive, design, mental feeling, pain, and bodily health), but not including a statement of memory or belief to prove the fact remembered or believed unless it relates to the execution, revocation, identification, or terms of declarant's will.

(4) Statements for Purposes of Medical Diagnosis or Treatment. Statements made for purposes of medical diagnosis or treatment and describing medical history, or past or present symptoms, pain, or sensations, or the inception or general character of the cause or external source thereof insofar as reasonably pertinent to diagnosis or treatment.

(5) Recorded Recollection. A memorandum or record concerning a matter about which a witness once had knowledge but now has insufficient recollection to enable the witness to testify fully and accurately, shown to have been made or adopted by the witness when the matter was fresh in the witness' memory and to reflect that knowledge correctly. If admitted, the memorandum or record may be read into evidence but may not itself be received as an exhibit unless offered by an adverse party.

(6) Records of Regularly Conducted Activity. (Reserved. See RCW 5.45.)

(7) Absence of Entry in Records Kept in Accordance With RCW 5.45. Evidence that a matter is not included in the memoranda, reports, records, or data

compilations, in any form, kept in accordance with the provisions of RCW 5.45, to prove the nonoccurrence or nonexistence of the matter, if the matter was of a kind of which a memorandum, report, record, or data compilation was regularly made and preserved, unless the sources of information or other circumstances indicate lack of trustworthiness.

(8) Public Records and Reports. (Reserved. See RCW 5.44.040.)

(9) Records of Vital Statistics. Records or data compilations, in any form, of births, fetal deaths, deaths, or marriages, if the report thereof was made to a public office pursuant to requirements of law.

(10) Absence of Public Record or Entry. To prove the absence of a record, report, statement, or data compilation, in any form, or the nonoccurrence or nonexistence of a matter of which a record, report, statement, or data compilation, in any form, was regularly made and preserved by a public office or agency, evidence in the form of a certification in accordance with rule 902, or testimony, that diligent search failed to disclose the record, report, statement, or data compilation, or entry.

(11) Records of Religious Organizations. Statements of births, marriages, divorces, deaths, legitimacy, ancestry, relationship by blood or marriage, or other similar facts of personal or family history, contained in a regularly kept record of a religious organization.

(12) Marriage, Baptismal, and Similar Certificates. Statements of fact contained in a certificate that the maker performed a marriage or other ceremony or administered a sacrament, made by a clergyman, public official, or other person authorized by the rules or practices of a religious organization or by law to perform the act certified, and purporting to have been

issued at the time of the act or within a reasonable time thereafter.

(13) Family Records. Statements of fact concerning personal or family history contained in family Bibles, genealogies, charts, engravings on rings, inscriptions on family portraits, tattoos, engravings on urns, crypts, or tombstones, or the like.

(14) Records of Documents Affecting an Interest in Property. The record of a document purporting to establish or affect an interest in property, as proof of the content of the original recorded document and its execution and delivery by each person by whom it purports to have been executed, if the record is a record of a public office and an applicable statute authorized the recording of documents of that kind in that office.

(15) Statements in Documents Affecting an Interest in Property. A statement contained in a document purporting to establish or affect an interest in property if the matter stated was relevant to the purpose of the document unless dealings with the property since the document was made have been inconsistent with the truth of the statement or the purport of the document.

(16) Statements in Ancient Documents. Statements in a document in existence 20 years or more whose authenticity is established.

(17) Market Reports, Commercial Publications. Market quotations, tabulations, lists, directories, or other published compilations, generally used and relied upon by the public or by persons in particular occupations.

(18) Learned Treatises. To the extent called to the attention of an expert witness upon cross examination

or relied upon by the expert witness in direct examination, statements contained in published treatises, periodicals, or pamphlets on a subject of history, medicine, or other science or art, established as a reliable authority by the testimony or admission of the witness or by other expert testimony or by judicial notice. If admitted, the statements may be read into evidence but may not be received as exhibits.

(19) Reputation Concerning Personal or Family History. Reputation among members of a person's family by blood, adoption, or marriage, or among a person's associates, or in the community, concerning a person's birth, adoption, marriage, divorce, death, legitimacy, relationship by blood, adoption, or marriage, ancestry, or other similar fact of a person's personal or family history.

(20) Reputation Concerning Boundaries or General History. Reputation in a community, arising before the controversy, as to boundaries of or customs affecting lands in the community, and reputation as to events of general history important to the community or state or nation in which located.

(21) Reputation as to Character. Reputation of a person's character among his associates or in the community.

(22) Judgment of Previous Conviction. Evidence of a final judgment, entered after a trial or upon a plea of guilty (but not upon a plea of nolo contendere), adjudging a person guilty of a crime punishable by death or imprisonment in excess of 1 year, to prove any fact essential to sustain the judgment, but not including, when offered by the prosecution in a criminal case for purposes other than impeachment, judgments against persons other than the accused. The pendency of an appeal may be shown but does not affect admissibility.

(23) Judgment as to Personal, Family, or General History, or Boundaries. Judgments as proof of matters of personal, family, or general history, or boundaries, essential to the judgment, if the same would be provable by evidence of reputation.

(b) Other Exceptions. (Reserved.)


[Amended effective September 1, 1992.]


Comment 803

[Deleted effective September 1, 2006.]


## RULE ER 804. HEARSAY EXCEPTIONS; DECLARANT UNAVAILABLE


(a) Definition of Unavailability. "Unavailability as a witness" includes situations in which the declarant:

(1) Is exempted by ruling of the court on the ground of privilege from testifying concerning the subject matter of the declarant's statement; or

(2) Persists in refusing to testify concerning the subject matter of the declarant's statement despite an order of the court to do so; or

(3) Testifies to a lack of memory of the subject matter of the declarant's statement; or

(4) Is unable to be present or to testify at the hearing because of death or then existing physical or mental illness or infirmity; or

(5) Is absent from the hearing and the proponent of the statement has been unable to procure the declarant's attendance (or in the case of a hearsay exception under subsection (b)(2), (3), or (4), the declarant's attendance or testimony) by process or other reasonable means.

(6) A declarant is not unavailable as a witness if the exemption, refusal, claim of lack of memory, inability, or absence is due to the procurement or wrongdoing of the proponent of a statement for the purpose of preventing the witness from attending or testifying.

(b) Hearsay Exceptions. The following are not excluded by the hearsay rule if the declarant is unavailable as a witness:

(1) Former Testimony. Testimony given as a witness at another hearing of the same or a different proceeding, or in a deposition taken in compliance with law in the course of the same or another proceeding, if the party against whom the testimony is now offered, or, in a civil action or proceeding, a predecessor in interest, had an opportunity and similar motive to develop the testimony by direct, cross, or redirect examination.

(2) Statement Under Belief of Impending Death. In a trial for homicide or in a civil action or proceeding, a statement made by a declarant while believing that the declarant's death was imminent, concerning the cause or circumstances of what the declarant believed to be the declarant's impending death.

(3) Statement Against Interest. A statement which was at the time of its making so far contrary to the declarant's pecuniary or proprietary interest, or so far tended to subject the declarant to civil or

criminal liability, or to render invalid a claim by the declarant against another, that a reasonable person in the declarant's position would not have made the statement unless the person believed it to be true. In a criminal case, a statement tending to expose the declarant to criminal liability is not admissible unless corroborating circumstances clearly indicate the trustworthiness of the statement.

(4) Statement of Personal or Family History. (i) A statement concerning the declarant's own birth, adoption, marriage, divorce, legitimacy, relationship by blood, adoption, or marriage, ancestry, or other similar fact of personal or family history, even though declarant had no means of acquiring personal knowledge of the matter stated; or (ii) a statement concerning the foregoing matters, and death also, of another person, if the declarant was related to the other by blood, adoption, or marriage or was so intimately associated with the others family as to be likely to have accurate information concerning the matter declared.

(5) Other Exceptions. (Reserved.)

(6) Forfeiture by wrongdoing. A statement offered against a party that has engaged directly or indirectly in wrongdoing that was intended to, and did, procure the unavailability of the declarant as a witness.


[Amended effective September 1, 1992; September 1, 2013.]


Comment 804


[Deleted effective September 1, 2006.]

Hearsay included within hearsay is not excluded under the hearsay rule if each part of the combined statements conforms with an exception to the hearsay rule provided in these rules.

[Adopted effective April 2, 1979.]

Comment 805

[Deleted effective September 1, 2006.]

## RULE ER 806. ATTACKING AND SUPPORTING CREDIBILITY OF DECLARANT

When a hearsay statement, or a statement defined in rule 801(d)(2)(iii), (iv), or (v), has been admitted in evidence, the credibility of the declarant may be attacked, and if attacked may be supported, by any evidence which would be admissible for those purposes if declarant had testified as a witness. Evidence of a statement or conduct by the declarant at any time, inconsistent with the declarant's hearsay statement, is not subject to any requirement that the declarant may have been afforded an opportunity to deny or explain. If the party against whom a hearsay statement has been admitted calls the declarant as a witness, the party is entitled to examine the declarant on the statement as if under cross examination.

[Amended effective September 1, 1992.]

Comment 806

[Deleted effective September 1, 2006.]

(Reserved. See RCW 9A.44.120.)

[Adopted effective September 1, 1988.]

Comment 807

[Deleted effective September 1, 2006.]

(a) General Provision. The requirement of authentication or identification as a condition precedent to admissibility is satisfied by evidence sufficient to support a finding that the matter in question is what its proponent claims.

(b) Illustrations. By way of illustration only, and not by way of limitation, the following are examples of authentication or identification conforming with the requirements of this rule:

(1) Testimony of Witness With Knowledge. Testimony that a matter is what it is claimed to be.

(2) Nonexpert Opinion on Handwriting. Nonexpert opinion as to the genuineness of handwriting, based upon familiarity not acquired for purposes of the litigation.

(3) Comparison by Court or Expert Witness. Comparison by the court or by expert witnesses with specimens which have been authenticated.

(4) Distinctive Characteristics and the Like. Appearance, contents, substance, internal patterns, or other distinctive characteristics, taken in conjunction with circumstances.

(5) Voice Identification. Identification of a voice, whether heard firsthand or through mechanical or electronic transmission or recording, by opinion based upon hearing the voice at any time under circumstances connecting it with the alleged speaker.

(6) Telephone Conversations. Telephone conversations, by evidence that a call was made to the

number assigned at the time by the telephone company to a particular person or business, if (i) in the case of a person, circumstances, including self-identification, show the person answering to be the one called, or (ii) in the case of a business, the call was made to a place of business and the conversation related to business reasonably transacted over the telephone.

(7) Public Records or Reports. (Reserved. See RCW 5.44 and CR 44.) (8) Ancient Documents or Data Compilation. Evidence that a document or data compilation, in any form, (i) is in such condition as to create no suspicion concerning its authenticity, (ii) was in a place where it, if authentic, would likely be, and (iii) has been in existence 20 years or more at the time it is offered.

(9) Process or System. Evidence describing a process or system used to produce a result and showing that the process or system produces an accurate result.

(10) Electronic Mail (E-mail). Testimony by a person with knowledge that (i) the e-mail purports to be authored or created by the particular sender or the sender's agent; (ii) the e-mail purports to be sent from an e-mail address associated with the particular sender or the sender's agent; and (iii) the appearance, contents, substance, internal patterns, or other distinctive characteristics of the e-mail, taken in conjunction with the circumstances, are sufficient to support a finding that the e-mail in question is what the proponent claims.

(11) Methods Provided by Statute or Rule. Any method of authentication or identification provided by statute or court rule.

[Adopted effective April 2, 1979; amended effective December 10, 2013.]

Comment 901

[Deleted effective September 1, 2006.]

## RULE ER 902. SELF-AUTHENTICATION

Extrinsic evidence of authenticity as a condition precedent to admissibility is not required with respect to the following:

(a) Domestic Public Documents Under Seal. A document bearing a seal purporting to be that of the United States, or of any state, district, commonwealth, territory, or insular possession thereof, or the Panama Canal Zone, or the Trust Territory of the Pacific Islands, or of a political subdivision, department, officer, or agency thereof, and a signature purporting to be an attestation or execution.

(b) Domestic Public Documents Not Under Seal. A document purporting to bear the signature in the official capacity of an officer or employee of any entity included in section (a), having no seal, if a public officer having a seal and having official duties in the district or political subdivision of the officer or employee certifies under seal that the signer has the official capacity and that the signature is genuine.

(c) Foreign Public Documents. A document purporting to be executed or attested in an official capacity by a person authorized by the laws of a foreign country to make the execution or attestation, and accompanied by a final certification as to the genuineness of the signature and official position (1) of the executing or attesting person, or (2) of any foreign official whose certificate of genuineness of signature and official position relates to the execution or attestation or is in a chain of certificates of genuineness of signature and official position relating to the execution or attestation. A final certification may be made by a secretary of embassy or legation, consul general, consul, vice-consul, or consular agent of the United States, or a diplomatic or consular official of the foreign country assigned or accredited to the United States. If reasonable opportunity has been given to all parties to investigate the authenticity and accuracy of official documents, the court may, for good cause shown, order that they be treated as presumptively authentic without final certification or permit them to be evidenced by an attested summary with or without final certification.

(d) Certified Copies of Public Records. A copy of an official record or report or entry therein, or of a document authorized by law to be recorded or filed and actually recorded or filed in a public office, including data compilations in any form, certified as correct by the custodian or other person authorized to make the certification, by certificate complying with section (a), (b), or (c) of this rule or complying with any applicable law, treaty or convention of the United States, or the applicable law of a state or territory of the United States.

(e) Official Publications. Books, pamphlets, or other publications purporting to be issued by public authority.

(f) Newspapers and Periodicals. Printed materials purporting to be newspapers or periodicals.

(g) Trade Inscriptions and the Like. Inscriptions, signs, tags, or labels purporting to have been affixed in the course of business and indicating ownership, control, or origin.

(h) Acknowledged Documents. Documents accompanied by a certificate of acknowledgment executed in the manner provided by law by a notary public or other officer authorized by law to take acknowledgments.

(i) Commercial Paper and Related Documents. Commercial paper, signatures thereon, and documents relating thereto to the extent provided by general commercial law.

(j) Presumptions Created by Law. Any signature, document, or other matter declared by any law of the United States or of this state to be presumptively or prima facie genuine or authentic.

[Amended effective August 27, 1980; September 1, 1988; September 1, 1992.]

Comment 902

[Deleted effective September 1, 2006.]

## RULE ER 903. SUBSCRIBING WITNESS' TESTIMONY UNNECESSARY

The testimony of a subscribing witness is not necessary to authenticate a writing unless required by the laws of the jurisdiction whose laws govern the validity of the writing.

[Adopted effective April 2, 1979.]

Comment 903

[Deleted effective September 1, 2006.]

(a) Certain Documents Admissible. In a civil case, any of the following documents proposed as exhibits in accordance with section (b) of this rule shall be deemed admissible unless objection is made under section (c) of this rule:

(1) A bill, report made for the purpose of treatment, chart, record of a hospital, doctor, dentist, registered nurse, licensed practical nurse, physical therapist, psychologist or other health care provider, on a letterhead or billhead;

(2) A bill for drugs, medical appliances or other related expenses on a letterhead or billhead;

(3) A bill for, or an estimate of, property damage on a letterhead or billhead. In the case of an estimate, the party intending to offer the estimate shall forward a copy to the adverse party with a statement indicating whether or not the property was repaired, and if it was, whether the estimated repairs were made in full or in part and attach a copy of the receipted bill showing the items of repair and amounts paid;

(4) A weather or traffic signal report, or standard United States government table;

(5) A photograph, x-ray, drawing, map, blueprint or similar documentary evidence;

(6) A document not specifically covered by any of the foregoing provisions but relating to a material fact and having equivalent circumstantial guaranties of trustworthiness, the admission of which would serve the interests of justice.

(b) Notice. Any party intending to offer a document under this rule must serve on all parties a notice, no less than 30 days before trial, stating that the documents are being offered under Evidence Rule 904 and shall be deemed authentic and admissible without testimony or further identification, unless objection is served within 14 days of the date of notice, pursuant to ER 904(c). The notice shall be accompanied by (1) numbered copies of the documents and (2) an index, which shall be organized by document number and which shall contain a brief description of the document along with the name, address and telephone number of the document's author or maker. The notice shall be filed with the court. Copies of documents that accompany the notice shall not be filed with the court.

(c) Objection to Authenticity or Admissibility. Within 14 days of notice, any other party may serve on all parties a written objection to any document offered under section (b), identifying each document to which objection is made by number and brief description.

(1) If an objection is made to a document on the basis of authentication, and if the court finds that the objection was made without reasonable basis, the offering party shall be entitled to an award of expenses and reasonable attorney fees incurred as a result of the required proof of authentication as to each such document determined to be authentic and offered as an exhibit at the time of trial.

(2) If an objection is made to a document on the basis of admissibility, the grounds for the objection shall be specifically set forth, except objection on the grounds of relevancy need not be made until trial. If the court finds that the objection was made without reasonable basis and the document is admitted as an exhibit at trial, the court may award the offering party any expenses incurred and reasonable attorney fees.

(d) Effect of Rule. This rule does not restrict argument or proof relating to the weight to be accorded the evidence submitted, nor does it restrict the trier of fact's authority to determine the weight of the evidence after hearing all of the evidence and the arguments of opposing parties.

[Adopted effective September 18, 1992; amended effective October 29, 1993; January 27, 1998.]

For purposes of this article the following definitions are applicable:

(a) Writings and Recordings. "Writings" and "recordings" consist of letters, words, sounds, or numbers, or their equivalent, set down by handwriting, typewriting, printing, photostating, photographing, magnetic impulse, mechanical or electronic recording, or other form of data compilation.

(b) Photographs. "Photographs" include still photographs, X-ray films, videotapes, and motion pictures.

(c) Original. An "original" of a writing or recording is the writing or recording itself or any counterpart intended to have the same effect by a person executing or issuing it. An "original" of a photograph includes the negative or any print therefrom. If data are stored in a computer or similar device, any printout or other output readable by sight, shown to reflect the data accurately, is an "original".

(d) Duplicate. A "duplicate" is a counterpart produced by the same impression as the original, or from the same matrix, or by means of photography, including enlargements and miniatures, or by mechanical or electronic recording, or by chemical reproduction, or by other equivalent techniques which accurately reproduce the original.

[Amended effective August 27, 1980.]

Comment 1001

[Deleted effective September 1, 2006.]

## RULE ER 1002. REQUIREMENT OF ORIGINAL

To prove the content of a writing, recording, or photograph, the original writing, recording, or photograph is required, except as otherwise provided in these rules or by rules adopted by the Supreme Court of this state or by statute.

Comment 1002

[Deleted effective September 1, 2006.]

## RULE ER 1003. ADMISSIBILITY OF DUPLICATES

A duplicate is admissible to the same extent as an original unless (1) a genuine question is raised as to the authenticity of the original or (2) in the circumstances it would be unfair to admit the duplicate in lieu of the original.

Comment 1003

[Deleted effective September 1, 2006.]

## RULE ER 1004. ADMISSIBILITY OF OTHER EVIDENCE OF CONTENTS

The original is not required, and other evidence of the contents of a writing, recording, or photograph is admissible if:

(a) Original Lost or Destroyed. All originals are lost or have been destroyed, unless the proponent lost or destroyed them in bad faith; or

(b) Original Not Obtainable. No original can be obtained by any available judicial process or procedure; or

(c) Original in Possession of Opponent. At a time when an original was under the control of the party against whom offered, that party was put on notice, by the pleadings or otherwise, that the contents would be a subject of proof at the hearing, and that party does not produce the original at the hearing; or

(d) Collateral Matters. The writing, recording, or photograph is not closely related to a controlling issue.

Comment 1004

[Deleted effective September 1, 2006.]

## RULE ER 1005. PUBLIC RECORDS

The contents of an official record, or of a document authorized to be recorded or filed and actually recorded or filed, including data compilations in any form, if otherwise admissible, may be proved by copy, certified as correct in
accordance with rule 902 or testified to be correct by a witness who has compared it with the original. If a copy which complies with the foregoing cannot be obtained by the exercise of reasonable diligence, then other evidence of the contents may be given.

Comment 1005

[Deleted effective September 1, 2006.]


## RULE ER 1006. SUMMARIES


The contents of voluminous writings, recordings, or photographs which cannot conveniently be examined in court may be presented in the form of a chart, summary, or calculation. The originals, or duplicates, shall be made available for examination or copying, or both, by other parties at reasonable time and place. The court may order that they be produced in court.


Comment 1006

[Deleted effective September 1, 2006.]

## RULE ER 1007. TESTIMONY OR WRITTEN ADMISSION OF PARTY


Contents of writings, recordings, or photographs may be proved by the testimony or deposition of the party against whom offered or by that party's written admission, without accounting for the nonproduction of the original.


Comment 1007

[Deleted effective September 1, 2006.]

## RULE ER 1008. FUNCTIONS OF COURT AND JURY

When the admissibility of other evidence of contents of writings, recordings, or photographs under these rules depends upon the fulfillment of a condition of fact, the question whether the condition has been fulfilled is ordinarily for the court to determine in accordance with the provisions of rule 104. However, when an issue is raised (1) whether the asserted writing ever existed, or (2) whether another writing, recording, or photograph produced at the trial is the original, or (3) whether other evidence of contents correctly reflects the contents, the issue is for the trier of fact to determine as in the case of other issues of fact.

Comment 1008

[Deleted effective September 1, 2006.]

(a)   Courts Generally. Except as otherwise provided in section (c), these rules apply to all actions and proceedings in the courts of the state of Washington. The terms "judge" and "court" in these rules refer to any judge of any court to which these rules apply or any other officer who is authorized by law to hold any hearing to which these rules apply.

(b)   Law With Respect to Privilege. The law with respect to privileges applies at all stages of all actions, cases, and proceedings.

(c)   When Rules Need Not Be Applied. The rules (other than with respect to privileges, the rape shield statute and ER 412) need not be applied in the following situations:

(1)   Preliminary Questions of Fact. The determination of questions of fact preliminary to admissibility of evidence when the issue is to be determined by the court under rule 104(a).

(2)   Grand Jury. Proceedings before grand juries and special inquiry judges.

(3)   Miscellaneous Proceedings. Proceedings for extradition or rendition; detainer proceedings under RCW 9.100; preliminary determinations in criminal cases; sentencing, or granting or revoking probation; issuance of warrants for arrest, criminal summonses, and search warrants; proceedings with respect to release on bail or otherwise; contempt proceedings in which the court may act summarily; habeas corpus proceedings; small claims court; supplemental proceedings under RCW 6.32; coroners' inquests; preliminary determinations in juvenile court; juvenile

court hearings on declining jurisdiction; disposition, review, and permanency planning hearings in juvenile court; dispositional determinations related to treatment for alcoholism, intoxication, or drug addiction under RCW 70.96A; and dispositional determinations under
RCW 71.05 and 71.34.

(4) Applications for Protection Orders. Protection order proceedings under Chapters 7.90, 7.92, 7.94, 10.14, 26.50, and 74.34 RCW. Provided when a judge proposes to consider information from a criminal or civil database, the judge shall disclose the information to each party present at the hearing; on timely request, provide each party with an opportunity to be heard; and take appropriate measures to alleviate litigants' safety concerns. The judge has discretion not to disclose information that he or she does not propose to consider.

(d) Arbitration Hearings. In a mandatory arbitration hearing under RCW 7.06, the admissibility of evidence is governed by MAR 5.3.


[Adopted effective April 2, 1979. Amended effective January 1, 1980; August 27, 1980; September 1, 1989; September 1, 1992; September 21, 1999; January 2, 2008; September 1, 2008, September 1, 2010; December 10, 2013; May 27, 2014; December 8, 2015; July 4, 2017.]


Comment 1101

[Deleted effective September 1, 2006.]

## RULE ER 1102. AMENDMENTS

(RESERVED)

These rules may be known and cited as the Washington Rules of Evidence.
ER is the official abbreviation.

[Effective April 2, 1979.]